A Choice of Dreams

A Choice of Dreams

Joy Kogawa

McClelland and Stewart Limited

0-7710-4526-3

The Canadian Publishers
McClelland and Stewart Limited
25 Hollinger Road, Toronto

Printed and bound in Canada

Acknowledgements

Prism international, West Coast Review, Quarry, Chicago Review, *Forty Women Poets of Canada,* The Literary Half Yearly, *Toboggans and Turtlenecks,* Canadian Forum, Fiddlehead, Edge, C.B.C. Anthology. "Dear Euclid" was presented as a dramatised monologue by the University of Ottawa Drama Guild workshop, adapted and directed by Jeremy Gibson, in November 1971.

Contents

About Japan

Ancestor's Graves in Kurakawa

Down down across the open sea to Shikoku
To story book island of mist and mystery
By train and bus through remote mountain villages
Following my father's boyhood backwards
Retracing the mountain path he crossed on rice husk slippers
With his dreams of countries beyond seas beyond seas
His dreams still intact, his flight perpetual
Back down the steep red mountain path
To the high hillside grave of my ancestors
Grey and green ferns hang down
Edging my faint beginnings with shades
Maintaining muteness in a wordless flickering
The hiddenness stretches beyond my reach
Strange dew drops through cedar incense
And I greet the dead who smile through trees
Accepting the pebbles that melt through my eyes.

On Flight 401

Sea blue stewardess with celluloid limbs
Emerges through a focus of recorded words
Points one lilting fingertip
To metal compartments above
Sniffs an oxygen tube yellowy flower
Lowers a fashion show life raft

The ocean orchestrates her ballet
The air crash as distant as
The sound of the white spray

Descent into Smog

Bumpy chowder clouds our descent
Into forecast of smoke haze
Sun angles away to airport scene
The Tokyo trot
Much bowing, many bow legs
A grey kimono emerges, tightness, anxiety—
My aunt has helmetitis, or is it
Just a temporary helmet she puts on
When something has to be done—
Like walking under ladders
Standing in hard hat areas
Meeting North American strangers—
She asks hard hat questions:
What's your name, girl? Curiosa?
Cursiosa? Schedule, purpose
What's your game?
Home is where the heart is, I feel
Which is an open question
These wounding days.
She escorts me through black exhaust
Hurtling smog, open toilet smells
Jerky conversation, I cut the automatic
And turn to manual breathing, watch the
Red alert in my temple and
Try to adjust.

Street Corner, Tokyo

A cluster of hippies
Flowers of plastic bags gripped to their noses
Inhale themselves off the island
To places hazy as drift cloud
Plastered with paint thinner

A farmer totters by on geta
Swallows his sakë and is swallowed
Into the bloodstream, a droplet
Dripping into the world's liver

An artist paints a dusty tree
Assigns his signature
To a falling leaf

Zen Graveyard

Thick night mist
Mountainside, stone ghosts, graves
Rising in steps into trees
Strange familiarity
Small girl once upon a time
Red and white kimono, short hair
Not here perhaps but somewhere
A wild boar perhaps, perhaps not
Waterfall, a sound not unlike a violin
Bell tone of insect, praying mantis nearby
Curled coloured snails on mossy trees—
To have to stand alone here
In this almost place when
Once upon a time, perhaps—

On Hearing Japanese Haiku

Throat blossoms to sounds
Sama zama no mono
Stirrings in the sandy fibres of my flesh
And these ancient fingers
Gardening

A Tempo

Lost in a maze of corridors
With a useless map
Streets the width of hallways
And basin size backyard gardens
Bow legged women churn the
Everywhere falling dust
Brown air brown arms brown earth
A piano player plays a Bach fugue
With the piano
Almost on the sidewalk
A patchy rooster
Squats in a cramped cage

Glances

At first glance I am in a no-shout, no-spank
Network of sensitivity training course graduates,
The only reprimand being "Everyone is watching you."
Fierce eyes, fearful eyes are more than enough
And shame is the public watchdog.

At second glance I notice tiny pock mark scars
On the back of a lady's hand and remember
That peculiar old Japanese punishment
Of setting a sen sen size square to smoulder
And burn a brand on the naughty child's skin—
A strange code of barely discernible public glances
And private barbarisms—a constant inconsistency
And multi-standard code of behaviour.

By the fifth and sixth glances I come to a tangle
Of subtleties, stomach ulcers and suicides
And I surface for air in an art gallery.
On one wall hangs an outline of a pot in red
With the English word POT printed in green.
A thin line borders the picture
With dimensions in neat Roman numerals
Marked in the lower right corner.

At first glance I am drained of subtlety
But by the fifty and sixth glances
I am fleeing the art gallery
To watch a tea ceremony
Where guests empty their minds
As they empty the contents of ancient rustic tea bowls.
At first glance the tea ceremony
Seems a tedious discipline fit for old ladies.

This Is a Clearing

This is a clearing
There is the forest
This is the forest
There is the clearing.
My gentle relatives are standing in dark sunlight
Whispered about with monumental propriety
Gathering on the occasion of a wedding
To impale and dismember a missing relative
Chanting a creed "We belong. We belong."
I stand on the edge
If I enter the forest I am lost
If I enter the clearing I am still lost
I move in a direction
Chanting a creed, "We belong. We belong."
A large tree cracks

On Meeting the Clergy
of the Holy Catholic Church in Osaka

Heralded into a belly swelling bladder bloating banquet
Where the excessive propriety is hard on the digestion
Elegant ladies in kimonos and holy men with holier manners
Bow and re-bow in strict pecking order
Munch the meal and mouth polite belching and
Rush at flood tide to the integrated toilet
Where men still proper and black suited in a row
Stand toes out and eyes down in syncopated gush
While ladies in kimonos mince by without blush or bellow
And I follow snuffling to hide a guffaw though
Why I should laugh—which reminds me
At the Osaka zoo my friend kept pointing out
The peeing fox and the baboon's purple bum and such
Asking how to say these things in English
And I tried to explain about the odd Canadians
Who have no bread and butter words
To describe these ordinary things.

For the Annual Service of Thanks
that Kyoto Was Spared the Bomb

For the fact that this temple was not bombed
And these dragons still stand guard—
For this network of lanes on the city's edges
Shaded by ancient trees
For this pre-Meiji pond and its family of rocks
This still living and aging thatch roofed house
For Kinkakuji and Ginkakuji and countless wooden buildings
For these and other treasures still preserved
We give thanks o military strategists
And wish a happy unbirthday to you Kyoto,
Pollyanna city of grace and gratitude.
A few miles away in Hiroshima
The wide boulevard in front of Peace Park
Is jammed on International Peace Day
With a new generation of students
Who feel they know what to say.

The Chicken Killing

Down the dusty country lane
Along drying rice propped in lines like soldiers on parade
And blue pantalooned people in the distance pantomiming—
Two men standing, three crouched in ritual stance
Sweat cloths around foreheads, open undershirts, black cloth boots
One with knife, one grinning toothless—
Plump white fluttering held feet first
Conveniently drains its veins as it struggles
Then flung aside, leaps through the air—
I walk past down the trembling road
Tasting the sound of dusty feet and
Feeling on my neck the slight saltiness of a question—
I am dangling feet first from the sky
—Perhaps if I do not struggle—

Public Bath

Daily to the ofuro
With basin, soap, towel and thirty-five yen
With neighbours strangers and friends
To boil away altogether
All together in the bath
And with wash cloth rolled tight
As hard ball pumice stone
Scrape and scrub each other's backs
Already lobster red from steam
Squat and flob flob with soap
And splash and soak again
Till steam and dumpling soft
We merge as one warm vat
Of boiled jelly fish
All our offensive scabs and irritations
Rolled off in communal banter.
Would that this could be exported home
And politicians and business men and sons
Could meet together in the public bath
To batter and scrub each other raw
And dissolve the ills of the day
And my frozen neighbours in suburbia
Grannies and babies and mothers
And children all wrapped in skin
Could melt at the end of their day
In a warm soft body blending.

Saturday Night in Osaka

Strolling along the stretching Saturday night streets of Osaka
Between Osaka station and the dark corner of the YWCA
Jostled by mini car and multi-legged man
In narrow lane of lantern light and noise
Screeching brakes of unoiled bicycles
Pachinko parlors, glowing purple escalators
With my Japanese face in my dragon lady disguise
English like a dagger in my teeth
Flashing out against lonely challenging men
"Be my friend, Miss? Have some tea?"
Shrug. (I don't speak Japanese anyway, kid.)
I saunter back to the safety of the Y
And glumly brush my fangs with toothpaste
Like a million other antiseptic inhibited biddies
Who fear to look ridiculous or worse
And for the rest of the evening
Thumb through a Japanese-English dictionary
And listen to the man in the next alley
As he directs the traffic of a swaggering Saturday night
Shouting "Orai Orai Orai" (All right. All right.)
Among the centipedes and dragonflies and exploding neon lights.

Day of the Bride

The day of the bride dawns
Through layers of white plaster skin
And multi-sashed kimono
Head made huge by lacquered hair—
She is swept ashore in her glass bottle
White and tight as a folded paper message
Eyes hidden in a swirl of green boughs.
She moves like a mannequin
Manoeuvred by centuries of ceremony
Under the weight of speech and incantation
A wail of priests and watching families
Beside rows of low tables
With small triangles of paper
Congratulatory slits of squid and curls of seaweed.
Then kneeling at the bend of a fresh memory
She is discarded by her heavy day
And is plunged into the twentieth century
Tiny apartment daily stream
As a barely visible
Folded paper speck

Rush Hour Tokyo

Pelted shapeless in rush hour crush
As in a whash mash mochi making
A mad cab exhaust spot
Bicycle pedestrian car cart jostling
Hip to bumper, wheel to toe
Police whistle siren scream political
Speech radio singer neon I blur
Into this excess of faceless flesh rushing
Round this blender of glazed eyes—
Particle waves of people
Whip at typhoon speed past ticket takers
The world's most accurate mechanical men
And pummel up subway systems
Spew onto streets and platforms
Where demons within demons within demons
Riot for release or finale
Like staccato repetitions in frenzied fugues
Locked in a constant crescendo—
Canada oh my home and native land
Give me land lots of land don't
Fence don't fence me in—

Night in a Boat between Beppu and Kobe

At least three hundred men and five women
In the lower section of this rocking boat
Squeezed body to body on the thrumming floor
Some men fully dressed in underwear
Drinking sakë, playing cards and singing
Some already snoring open mouthed
Stiff on their backs beside each other
I squinch into my corner and lie down
Too curious to sleep too proper to be comfortable
The question of the unalert moment
Propping open my east-west eyes
A man's foot is on my buttock help
But he seems to be asleep
And I am watchtower
Witnessing on a busy corner
Sleepwalking with a pamphlet in my hand
That says Awake, Lick the crust from your eyelids
Watch and wait (it's a sightseeing trip)
I begin the taking off and putting on of masks
Smiling carefully at the man on my other side
And frowning at the demons dancing
Gleeing to my bright dark imaginings
By morning I am in a stupor
Having dramatized my corner all night
But can only report that there is no action
In having a strange man's foot on one's buttock
In a crowded overnight boat in Japan.
On the deck and in the first class cabins
Other passengers have been viewing
What some say is the world's
Most scenic inland sea.

Newspaper Item: Student Suicide

In soot silence, bamboo grows
Tree surgeons discuss the cause of wood rot
Pines point crooked arms to the sky

Rain drops the sky down in grey pieces and
Darkness moves with the urgency of flight
From a bad dream

Everyday
The newspaper reports
A bad dream

Tomorrows were mountaintops
Sculptured pines
And wind pruned asymmetry

A student went chestnut picking
And heard the "mim mim"
Of an autumn cicada.

Dwarf Trees

Out of the many small embarrassments of the day
Grew a miniature personality
Leafing itself gingerly in whatever genuine smile
It recognized in the thick undergrowth.
Dwarf trees planted in a fertile gentleness
Beside lush vegetation and sheltering green fans
Grew angular and stunted in a constant adjustment to cutting.
Horns of new growths sprouted
To bleed into warts and tiny anxieties.
Glances of disapproval felt as sharply
As salivating fangs tore at limbs.
Men developed into twisted sculptures of endurance
Bowing and smiling in civilized anger
And old women pruned daily into careful beauty
Glanced away in a cultivated shyness
Hiding smiles with humpbacked hands
Symbolizing by small gestures
Tiny treasures from a hidden childhood.

Lost Man at the Tourist Information Centre

Wide eyed and childlike the lost one comes
Bulbous nosed Australian, outstandingly fat
Flailing his stubby wings at all the strange
Bobbing creatures in his way.
Booms at the prim hostess
"I've been in Japan a fortnight
And haven't eaten a good Australian meal
I'm almost starving to death."
Japanese blinks at the bulk in front.
No mirth.
Clucking efficiency she flutters
On her perch at the Lost and Found booth
Roots through directories for the choicest grub
Bobs and bows the waddler on his way
Into the mad taxi traffic
Of the Ginza barnyard
Where he bellows like a baby ox
Lost in a forest of fragility
And intensely earnest jack-in-a-boxes
Doing abstract choreography.

School in the Woods

North Korean school in Kyoto woods, sports day
Blue white uniformed young people,
Military music, red star in white circle
A poster of a soldier wielding a long gun
Another of a toothy u.s. devil
Bayoneting an oriental man

A small boy in front of me eats a rice ball
And watches me with a careful stare
It is an autumn day in Kyoto
Full of tiny coloured maple leaves

Back home, some mother glimpses
Bayonets in the air, turns off the tv
Tucks her child into bed

Moon over Uchiko

9:00 p.m. evening lullaby and gong
Half hymn, half child's play song
Over this mountain village
Cicadas and crickets chirp whirr
Acorns drop down with soft thuds—
I slip through softly sliding doorways
Of matchstick wood and paper
To where my aunt in grey kimono
Sits in a rock garden by a pond
Beneath a white moon without hint of footprint.
Shuffling pigeon toed my aunt of much bowing
Descends upon my feet with great graciousness
Clutches my arms and clings parallel to earth
Suspended in the ether of my deciding
"Stay longer. Stay longer. Stay. Stay."
She opens for me her collection of memories
—My father as a child gathering cow dung for the garden
—My grandmother accused of farting in school
and weeping in a tub for a day—
She tugs me towards her dry hollows
And I am deformed with etiquette
As my plastic arms encircle her
And melt in the heat of her tears.
The steel beam in my back cracks
As she leans heavily crying and sighing.
I begin the countdown. Words to prop her
A cane for her to clutch. "Dear Aunt
I am beginning to learn how better to lie."
She bends double as I depart in a gust of metal
Rocketing the willowy trees bare in her October garden.

At Jindaiji Temple Fishing Pond

Rooting for the smooth grey fish
Being hooked and snared by laughing child
And powerless in the cool grey weather
To leap out of one element into another
Wishing only to avoid the death
Of being hooked on my gills by some cosmic child
And gleefully serenaded into a pebbly blackness
Of some gourmet's solar intestines—
Saying with vehemence I am a fish
And will die the death of a cold grey fish
Near my familiar mountain waterfall
But even here fishermen dangle
Worms on hooks into the stream of my peace
To pull me up into the rare foreign air.
Above the surface of my sky
Pure white seagulls circle
And I know that if I bite
It is for a devouring and an end
To the swift flash of my dark
Sporting body beneath the bumpy waves
But what does it matter to rot here or there
If I cannot will away this child
And the expansive smiling of his father.

Hiroshima Exit

In round round rooms of our wanderings
Victims and victimizers in circular flight
Fact pursuing fact
Warning leaflets still drip down
On soil heavy with flames,
Black rain, footsteps, witnessings—

The Atomic Bomb Memorial Building:
A curiosity shop filled with
Remnants of clothing, radiation sickness,
Fleshless faces, tourists muttering
"Well, they started it."
Words jingle down
"They didn't think about us in Pearl Harbor"
They? Us?
I tiptoe round the curiosity shop
Seeking my target
Precision becomes essential
Quick. Quick. Before he's out of range
Spell the name
America?
Hiroshima?
Air raid warnings wail bleakly
Hiroshima
Morning.
I step outside
And close softly the door
Believing, believing
That outside this store
Is another door

Insomnia in a Ryokan

What? No sound down the corridor?
No multiplicity of foot falls
Flap flap slippered slap
Or patter thud of plastic sole?
Only this foreign wooden floor
Only this faint echo of radio, tv, faraway drama
Flamenco dancers in dreams
Hints of snoring through hotel walls
What more can one ask?
A leap to a naked drum beat?
A primitive frenzy of touch?
One can insist on footsteps
One can insist on dancing
Look, the midnight can take shape
Slender fingerlings of dancing
Can cavort down corridors
Hah!
I'll leap into your snoring
Shout out my English subtitles
"Let me in!"
If you could understand my fairy tales

Holy Name Orphanage and Fukuse Byoin

The Holy Name Orphanage
Where an old blue hooded nun
Part eagle, part fish, feeds a baby
Her skinny intellectual hand
Holding a heavy spoon
She jerks his face frontwards
Shovel, jerk, shovel
He vomits finally
Small streams of mushy yellow
Down her blue skirt to the floor
She rises taller than she is
Avenging angel marching out
The baby watching her
And no longer intent on watching me.
I leave in an hour to visit
Fukuse Byoin at the foot of Mount Fuji—
A man skull faced and eaten away
After twenty years of Hansen's disease
Lies with sightless eyeballs perpetually bared
Bedridden, force fed, a gaping mouth
Uttering sounds in his constant night
A hallowe'en mask
I leave in an hour again
Walk the haunted city streets
Lady Macbeth, graduate tourist

Flower Arranger

Among the weedy steel structures
And frenetic flowering of factories
I found a blind flower arranger
In a sketch of a room
Dipping a drop of water
Onto an opening petal
Of a tiny not quite flowering bud.
With his fingertips
He placed gentleness in the air
And everywhere among the blowing weeds
He moved with his outstretched hands
Touching the air
With his transient dew.

Black Skirt of Mount Fuji in Rain

Almost late for the Tomei bus to Nagoya
Spot the one empty seat and sit down
By the bleary eyed man the others had shunned
He takes out his Suntory whisky, peels off
The plastic top, nudges me tentatively.
We travel on through several stages of misunderstanding
Me, anxious to see the countryside
And listening to the recorded announcements.
"Mount Fuji to the left" the voice says.
I peer out the window. Pouring rain.
The mountain exists in my imagination.
The next announcement. "I'm sorry
When you are in such a hurry
To have to stop for refuelling."
A lunchgirl arrives calling
"Bother is being done. Is lunch desired?"
Politeness all over this apologetic country
And I had to get old Suntory.
I decide to do a Mount Fuji
And obliterate myself in mist.
"Yes," I say in English to the nudger
"What would you like?"

Geisha

Invitations
dangle
from strings
like small
gem bead
curtains

eyes downcast
she steps through
and on her cheeks
are pink
flower
bruises

she paints
her sunsets
to match
his watching
and washes away
her mornings

Hangnail

Wondering about the importance of this hangnail
And its power over this massive hulk
Which dangles tenuously from its ledge
And this shuffling mass of a hangnail
From which the universe protrudes—
A hug might help
But I can't feel any cosmic arms
Nor earthly ones—
While walking I stepped on a giant moth
And in the long moment of its dying
All the accummulated injustices
Of squashed and battered bugs
Sacrificed on windshields
And sprayed to oblivion
Poured out of its eloquent wings
In one long fluttering—
And now the blood throbs in my thumb—
Attempting to atone the foot's misadventure?
Offering a salve of forgetfulness
To assuage my guilt?
An eye for an apple, a tooth for a pick
Kill the bugs if they make you sick—
The hangnail drones on interpreting itself
In the maze of my notions of justice
Which hang on as tenaciously and irritatingly
As a hangnail thread.

Dream after Touring the Tokyo Tokei

Electronic baby born to be
Guide in clock manufacturing hospital
Son of General Secretary of Resurrection
With a white bib on cold steel chest
Comes sliding squealing into this world
Ready to perform his single task
And guides me, ancient earthling
Through metal spot after metal spot
Where oil, like blood, alive, is flowing and
Small steel birds beep through the air
Carrying messages of cheer to the ill—
"Behold, before you were born I was here."
I reach out and am electrocuted
And the steel baby within me leaps—
Oh be born quickly before my flesh is Sarah grey
That I might see the shape of ancient promise

We step outside to Tokyo twentieth century
Seeds of slaves drift down from factory windows
And settle in the branches of dwarf trees
Settle on metal ledges and in the streets
Drop like confetti over the rose garden
And inside the bonnet of an opening rose
On the wrinkled old woman face of the bud
Stands a stiff black beetle on steely legs
An ancient wedding procession begins
In the dusty rose garden by the Tokyo Tokei.

Every spot is a sliding oil spot
And though I might seek to stay in this dream forever
I am sliding constantly in a procession.
Even at the moment of forgetting
An undercurrent has slid me further along.
Clandestine flesh and steel meetings
Move towards union
And beyond this another resurrection.

40

Goddess of Mercy

Autumn and not one leaf
On grey white sand, constant ripple
Of pebbly sea rock garden
The Goddess of Mercy rests her bronze ankle
On her knee, unmoving and perfect.
I slash the air like a medieval executioner
At a mosquito swooping past my face
And across the sand sea of eternity
Into the safety of the thick moss
My black blood in its belly.
Across the smoggy sky, two jets crisscross
From the highway a whine of traffic
Swells and fades

Girls in the Ginza

Bleach me brown or bleach me blonde
The Japanese girl demands
Surrounded by caucasian mannequins
Mocking oriental beauty.
She begs the plastic surgeon man
To snip the muscles of her slitty eyes
Lift her nose, plump her breasts—
False eyelashes and latest fashions on
She walks around the Ginza
Not quite who she wants to be
Her thick black hair rusting
Under the peroxide rain

Gift Giving and Obligation

Note from the lonely spaces:
Beware the kindness of the smother places
Where you are offered gift on gift.
Refuse carefully. Watch the eyes.
If they dart suddenly away from your glance
Smile and acknowledge the testing.
If the eyes murmur pleasure at your refusal
Refuse yet more profusely
Smiling with acceptance
Then condescend finally
Allowing and acknowledging
The superiority of gift giving.
Walk away burdened with an obligation
To continue exchanging for eternity
Complete with rituals of accumulating thankfulness
Or leave swiftly in the night
Before your neck is fastened with a whispering,
"Weight, weight, I love you."
Swim from the seaweed and strangulation
Westward to another island.

Child Eichmann

The orders were to kill the kittens
And obedience was the first commandment.
He took the first, still sac enclosed
A slippery blackness in his kitten size palm
And drowned it in a pail of water
Felt its pawing with needle thin scratchings
Watched it swimming, mewing, gaping—
Life comes, goes, mouths open, close,
The small sounds are buried in the night's
Darkness and wild dreaming. "Okaasan!"
She blames the persimmons and squats him
Over the open toilet which has not yet
Been cleaned by the monthly manure collector.
The smell from his bowels fills the house.

Bamboo Broom

At the Shinto shrine
Grey green stone lanterns
Scowling Chinese lion dogs
Protecting against irreverence and intrusion
Triangular tiny white porcelain foxes
Grains of rice placed at the feet
Of the rice god, Oinari-san
A record playing "Dinah won't you blow—"
A woman tossing a ten yen piece
Into a wooden box, bowing her head
Clapping her hands twice
Moss, water, tiny plum trees
PEACE cigarettes on the path
Another brand called HOPE
(Is there one called GOODWILL?)
A woman with a bamboo broom
Sweeping the ground
A tour of school children
In navy blue English uniforms
Crowding in past the lion dogs
(swish swish swish)

At Maruyama Park, Kyoto

Up stone steps to dark temple at night
A wail of flickering lights around stone statues
Centuries of looking down
Water drips, moss clings
A tiny brown frog leaps
Splash
Into a pool

At Shinjuku Park, November 19

Through the park
In autumn, warm leaf time
With transient foot
It being time to go home
Time, swear, to go home
And some loudspeaker plays
Auld Lang Syne
Yanking a raindrop out of nowhere.
We trudge through the song
Carrying the ocean with us.
Above us, seagulls cross
On a path of splashing waves
Brushing aside whatever spray
Clings to their wings
Their feathers filled with the buoyancy
Of those who love them.
Little point in delaying departure
Now the time to go has come
In the middle of this dance
In this autumn morning
I cling to my flight
While the rain
Gushes over my wings
And my goodbye face

Early Morning Stage

A messy city
Early morning and traffic whine mosquito whine
Toilet smell, cricket and dog sounds
Corrugated cardboard sheets
Oddly, a cow mooing? a rooster crowing?
The mosquito jabs my arm
I pull myself out of the heavy futon
Step over tatami to hallway
Slip on slip off slippers
Cloth slippers for hall
Plastic slippers for toilet
Squat foetal fashion over the flushless hole.
Through the floor level window vent
The sounds of feet pass
Outside in the pre-dawn grey and constant smog
Early morning scuttlers disappear
Pigeons flutter with the debris
A man with a fist full of red flowers
Urinates against a bush
A girl with an easel paints a school building
A loudspeaker above the school door plays
The "What a Friend We Have in Jesus" march
Bicycles with primitive brakes screech
Ladies hang futon over railings
A roast potato man
Pulls his wooden cart and calls
"Yaki imo" through his scratchy loudspeaker—

I remember that corner of Tokyo
But now I open my eyes
To a suburban white walled house in Ottawa
Early morning and a long silence
As if the curtain has just gone up
Or down and something electrifying has just happened
Or is about to happen and the day has begun
Or ended. It is up to me to decide
I am director producer playwright or
Actress on stage needing
Laughing lessons and I'm thinking
Of firing her. The audience has disappeared
And the walls intrude.
The mail truck crunches by.

Trunk in the Attic

Rummaging through the old metal trunk in
The attic above the church hall in Coaldale, Alberta—
The trunk which travelled with us
Through the World War 2 evacuation of Japanese
From the West Coast—filled then with dishes
Dresses and assorted treasures
And now only half full of baby dresses,
An old tablecloth, invitations to dinner Xmas 1915—
My white haired mother hands me
A deep purple kimono bought
In some vaguely remembered girlhood
Of apple shaped pears and sweet chestnuts
And utterly unabandoned babies
Asleep on their mothers' backs—
I take the memories from her tapered fingers
Fold her hands which no longer cling
Close the lid of the trunk.
The sharp whiff of mothballs fades from the room
And she turns to climb down the stairs
One step at a time
Rubbing the mucus steadily
From her cataract covered eyes.

Forest Creatures

When I Was a Little Girl

When I was a little girl
We used to walk together
Tim, my brother who wore glasses,
And I, holding hands
Tightly as we crossed the bridge
And he'd murmur, "You pray now"
—being a clergyman's son—
Until the big white boys
Had kicked on past.
Later we'd climb the bluffs
Overhanging the ghost town
And pick the small white lilies
And fling them like bombers
Over Slocan.

Breezes

The weeping willow sways low
In the breeze it seems to brush
The tops of those distant bushes
Sensuously in my one dimensional
Perception. Once I imagined
I knew so well the meaning
Of your careful words brushing
My mind gently with a nearness
Now I see how distant
The bushes are I still
Would paint them touching.

What Do I Remember of the Evacuation

What do I remember of the evacuation?
I remember my father telling Tim and me
About the mountains and the train
And the excitement of going on a trip.
What do I remember of the evacuation?
I remember my mother wrapping
A blanket around me and my
Pretending to fall asleep so she would be happy
Though I was so excited I couldn't sleep
(I hear there were people herded
Into the Hastings Park like cattle.
Families were made to move in two hours
Abandoning everything, leaving pets
And possessions at gun point.
I hear families were broken up
Men were forced to work. I heard
It whispered late at night
That there was suffering) and
I missed my dolls.
What do I remember of the evacuation?
I remember Miss Foster and Miss Tucker
Who still live in Vancouver

And who did what they could
And loved the children and who gave me
A puzzle to play with on the train.
And I remember the mountains and I was
Six years old and I swear I saw a giant
Gulliver of Gulliver's Travels scanning the horizon
And when I told my mother she believed it too
And I remember how careful my parents were
Not to bruise us with bitterness
And I remember the puzzle of Lorraine Life
Who said "Don't insult me" when I
Proudly wrote my name in Japanese
And Tim flew the Union Jack
When the war was over but Lorraine
And her friends spat on us anyway
And I prayed to the God who loves
All the children in his sight
That I might be white.

Chain Necklace

In my dream my mother wore
A necklace of small chains
Like a choker round her long neck
Which emphasized her beauty
And her swan like gracefulness
And in real life she made
Her choices, wore her chains
Kept her cygnets in the
Ugly barnyard world
Told me constantly to be
Gentle and to wear
The heavy chains with joy
But I grew squat and goose-like
And pick and jab my noose
At every chance.
My daughter takes the chains
Of daisies that I make
And twines them round our arms
But when I step aside
I learn that daisies bleed
Then slowly turn to steel.

Woodtick

The spring day the teen on his bike slanted his caucasian eyes
At my eight year old beautiful daughter
And taunted gibberish
I was eight years old and the Japs were
Enemies of Canada and the big white boys
And their golden haired sisters who
Lived in the ghost town of Slocan
Were walking together, crowding me
Off the path of the mountain, me running
Into the forest to escape
Into the pine brown and green lush dark
And getting lost and fearing woodticks
Which burrowed into your scalp beneath
Thick black hair follicles and could only be
Dug out by a doctor with hot needles—
Fearing sudden slips caused by melting snow
And steep ravines and the thick silence of
Steaming woods and cobwebs, so listening
For the guiding sound of their laughter
To lead me back to the path and
Following from a safe distance unseen
Till near the foot of the mountain
Then running past faster than their laughter
Home, vowing never to go again to the mountain
Alone—and Deidre whispers to walk faster
Though I tell her there are no
Woodticks in Saskatoon.

Forest Creatures

On this street there lives a little dark girl
A little dark girl with an orange coat
Black stockings and new shiny black shoes
Running to school through the mangled forest
One shiny new shoe flung away
By laughing boys with tiger faces—
Later my black haired daughter
Comes dancing home both shoes on
Replying, "Well she cheats when we play."
But tomorrow they are all together
Blue eyes, black hair, orange coat, tiger boys,
Skipping double dutch in the driveway
Colours all blending in a buttery chant.

Snakes

Suddenly in the woods a
Green and yellow snake as if he
Slithered down my back
A moving rope of wind slinking an instant
Barber shop sign round my spine
And as I clambered out of the woods—
Suddenly on the path a presence
Of children, one fearful whispering
"Chinese" and the other
Moving swiftly past—

Transplant

It's a matter of being
Uprooted by this gardener secretly
In the long dark night of my
Growing and planted in the
Sudden noon day trembling
Green house touch of his
Hands. Its a matter of blossoms
Exploding through the roots of my
Slow black hair and being
Trapped by the tendrils

Waterfall

In the space behind the waterfall
With that white sound background
On the cool rocks—
We lay there
Last night the pupils of your eyes
Were as large as Easter morning
The tunnel leading underground
And we were crouching
In the cave of our eyes
Our hands, water, flowing
Over the rock contours
Our hands, wings, blowing
The tombstone we
Heard the sound of sunrise
The flesh sound of word

Pray My Mantis

Dread this morning early and no
More sleeping. Awake to
Heavy summer tuneless song
The voice of mourning
Pray my lord mantis it
Is not so our green
Limbs an instant and the
Screeching birds over all

Flowering

The whole approach seems
Too young somehow
I mean—not because
Nudity is offensive, indeed
There is a glory in bronze
But I resent your insistence
That all must be tested by
The fire of our hot eyes.
Love flowers
When we deal gently
With shadows.

we were talking about stability

finally all the deceptions—
cloud, flight, departure
and i have said i do not
trust anymore but what
do i believe on this
plane? above? these clouds?
we are, i know, walking
on meringues and broken
egg shells, aren't we,
and trampling it all
solid—

finally that there is

no corner left in which to hide
the mouse, the cat
the empty room
the one defense left
is not to move at all
not to write
not to think
not to send you this letter

finally in the cat's jaws
i remember the secret door
listen for your tunnelling
realize finally that
you are the cat
you are the mouse
you are the room without doors
you are the secret tunnel

finally this fatal defense
fangs sharp with belief
back arched and clawing
the heart's walls

Tea Party

When birds dance for instance
Heads cocked, wings spread
Leaping back and forth, tearing turf
Instead of feathers

And we are polite and elegant
Sipping tea with steady hands
The wings beating beneath
Our ribs behind our eyes

Firebugs

We seemed to be seeking a
Mutual mugging, a double
Disintegration, we leapt over
The hanging cliff together
And fell with slow tenderness
In a consuming ballet an invisible
Hummingbird of hands and we talked
Of falling stars and the
Natural deaths on the rocks below
Our eyes faltering on the corniness
As the rocks shifted just enough
To show us the centre of the earth
Was still on fire and our soft
Avalanche gained bewilderment.

that we might not cling

a bird, you said, notice
how efficient it is twitching there
on the branch, chirping, eating and
crapping at the same time. and
disappearing too, i said

october 3

we were watching the ducks
in the middle of the river
the current swift as our blood
and the ducks
looking as if they were
not moving at all

we were as if
standing still watching the ducks
and he said
"should we fly south"

i said "yes"
and he talked about other things
while i stared at
the idiotic ducks

later there were
no ducks later
still no
river

South of Flin Flon, Highway 10

Two men fighting at Cranberry Portage
On the sidewalk, Sunday morning,
Choking, shouting, a silent crowd gathering,
Streaky faced children on cafe steps
Watching their elders
What else is there to do? Question
Do you tell it the way it is?
What is the way it is?
We in the car going by slowly to watch
The out of time story, we the out of place people.
Later on the highway we see a porcupine
Snout in air, outraged quills still quivering
Question. Is it dead? Is it suffering?
We say we don't know and keep driving
The car gradually picking up speed
Fleeing the weekend questions
The streaky faced children in the back seat
Finally growing silent and falling asleep.

Beach Poem

Walking in warm knee deep water
Watching tiny waves inside of waves
Inside of waves from hands and legs and
Bodies and boats and breeze
And making flat splashes, water leaping
In fat silver flashes to round circle bubbles
To float and pop and disappear forever
And repeating the flash and watching
The coming and going water pattern
And not seeing the round bald man
Who suddenly comes and splashes
And playfully grins yellow teeth
And grunts startlingly like a pig
And the water murky around him
And small pearly waters dripping
All around all around and I wish
I had a curly tail but sadly it is only forked

Rain Dance

Pestalozzi rainbow children in June storm
Deviant as ducklings in a chicken coop
Wings slapping naked skin
Under the window watching wire mesh
Hi yi yi yi Hi yi yi yi
Let it rain down let it rain
Clog the drains with dancing
Here are ark dwellers, dove senders
Mad as Noah

Porcupine

This is the way you are, Porcupine
I would wish you were otherwise
Gentle animal
Barricaded
Against my touch

Net

wait the net just
a minute why your
hands my throat your eyes my
fingers wait its a mistake all
this i only meant (hear me)
FRIENDSHIP
hear me your
hands a
sieve my words the
gills (hush) is it
only this (yes) i can
offer the
waves
the fins

The Girl Who Cried Wolf

"I love you" she said
"I do not lie."
 She showed him the slash in her arm.
"How can you sit there," she asked,
"Just sit there sit there."
"Because," he said, "it is the way of wolves."

Child Painting

A pink cloud, only
"At night," his black brush says
"You cannot see it
But it's still there moving
And tomorrow perhaps hail"
His brush grows roots
Flings branches skywards
A long black tree
Searching shapes
Enclosing clouds in a
Growing large
Black bird
"Tell me about your
Picture, Bobby."
Words are stones to birds in flight
His elbows move like wings.

Registration

Registration day was
Something like labour
All that waiting and
Walking and pushing and
Having finally registered
In one (1) *ONE*! course
I feel I've given birth
Successfully to a hamster

Tom Cat

The Tom cat comes calling Fluff
Meowering at the window
Though Fluff now hard ballooned
And weight flopping can't
Prance the cat call game
Fluff flops eyes narrowing contentment
Ignoring the ill timed serenade
Contemplating the kittens squishing her belly
And Tom trots off eventually

An alley cat, Tom and a piper's son
Eager for thievery with his tail
A swish this side of laughter
He shakes down fresh alleys
To a new pet shop kitten
The dry water velvet cling
Pussy cat fur of her
Curling round his thirsty skin
Raised in an alley of alternatives
Tom trots on continually

Biting Silences

The neat way they eat
Indicates nobility
But occasionally
They dine with pack rats
Fangs at the table are fine
Sometimes.

Afterwards, they burn my letters
In the fireplace.

Ants Are Taking Over

Ants are taking over my world
Woe to dancing grasshoppers
Beneath the concrete slab of my face
Ants are building tunnels
Neatly stock piling
Small grains of knowledge
At day's end the ants
Mount their mounds
Burrow through the pupils of my eyes
And giggle
At which point the ant smasher
With his midnight heel
Gouges a red hole in my concrete face.

Waiting Room

Waiting

A very quiet
        very quiet ticking
In the room where the child
Stays by the window
Watching
While outside innumerable snow feathers
Touch melt
      touch melt
          touch melt

Waiting Room

Midnight and the monks
Move down the corridor
"Dona nobis pacem"
The elves in the forest
The leaves breathing
Doctors, nurses
White in the moonlight—
Beneath a toppled toadstool
Clusters of ants carry white eggs
Struggle through collapsing tunnels

Three Dreams

1.
i rub the toy train on my sleeve
dusting it carefully
moving its wheels et cetera
wondering where the motor is
where the genie is

2.
on board the ship we find there are
many ways to cut the apple
to make the exquisite tiny ridges
for a special apple desert
it's the sort of thing that belongs
in a world without wars.

3.
she looks out the window
seeing the fire of the wars coming
we rush outside to rid ourselves
of poison. we vomit profusely
and make brown dung mounds
and this is our sole preparation

the day of lies approaches
if we tell all before the enemy comes
he will find the village emptied
and only the wind in the temple left
waiting to do him battle

how shall i tell of apples
in a world of wars

all the trees coloured were

all the trees coloured were
bird full and song ready to move
the forests alive with leaf swish and
ballet shoes on when suddenly
the 'no' storm fell cloud down
and curtain heavy i
cocoon the dark
                    grope
my fingernails black
the strange—
everywhere the strange
no colours left—

Rooster

Spear or smirk what does it matter
What the weapon is the wounds
Need tending need tenderness
What does it matter where the
Error lies when they
Come these days they
Come at once a
Rush of wounds and tenderness
With the rooster calling
His feet rooted in the night
His wings in the morning this is
Still the time
To forgive, to be forgiven

acceptance

a goliath of thoughts
about truth and schizophrenia
and your cowardice and my
judging you—i discover
david's stone was an avalanche
connected to this simple thing—
your truths are not mine and
it's okay

Dear Euclid

Moon announces at the end of my dream
"Dear Euclid
I am indestructible
I am star."

July. Thursday. 1971. New York.
From the airplane we drop
Ant powder on entire continents of bloodless ants
Like rain on Dolly's parade
The ticker tape confetti turning ash white
It's just a matter of time now
The cars crawling like paramecia
In drying drops

9:40. Sleepwalk into hot muggy New York
Stew people leaping from pot to pot
Swim through stop lights, computer talk
Please detach and retain this stub
For your personal use detach please
Your personal stub and retain your use
Do not fold staple or mutilate
Mold not do stupilate faple and
Give name age serial number
Ride up elevator. Salute. All that is
Tinier than Tom Thumb is not human
It is written on the screen of our understanding.
East Side Clinic. 11:00 a.m.

I had the choice—the dreamer has
His choice of dreams—I have
The choice still to turn about
In this tight tunnel ant corridor
Carrying my huge white ant egg
With all these other worker ants
Our antennae flashing urgency
The ground shaking our Soleri vision
City-in-a-building. The choice
Is still ours to protect our
City of the future, our rumbling eggs
In our shatterproof test tubes—the perspective
Is of our choosing and we are
Victim by choice, our victory only that
We can choose. What are we
Doing here, Toby, Sandra
Hiding from what menace, sharing our
Microscopic nightmare, offering these cells
These souls, these bodies, to be a reasonable
Holy and living sacrifice to whom for what?

Strange what surrenderings we regret
The sorrow of our bodies given
Strange what victories we retain
The sweetness of our bodies given
Yet that June night of battle
Neither victory nor loss was felt.
An act as non-passionate
As taking a sleeping pill on a restless night
And briefly your shadow leapt through
The dark red channels of pre-birth
Exploded star bright into incandescent life
Palpitated in a cosmos alive with expectation.

For how many days did you
Grow wildly hopeful until your heart
Barely beating in an entirely new sky
Died. Black. My star child. I would
Wish for you another age, another mother.

Once did God
Flood away his imperfect creation
And now the imperfection remains
And an ark full of regret.
My small Noah, it is to another world
You must go, not the
Vacuum aspirator, fast drying world
I walk on daily, not this
Morning and evening time heavy
Gasping to find laughter
Madness this dark mist stumbling.
I am Eskimo mother pursued by starving
Beasts by night and howling blizzard
And I abandon you, here, here, in the
White numbing coldness, your face I dare not
Look at for an instant longer, you are
Dead before you are alive and I don't know how
My limbs move when it is I
Should lie there with you, the foreign judge
Proclaiming my guilt and calling me
Murderer but my legs only frostbitten
Move on, stumbling in the perpetual winter

Farther away and farther always now to
Silences. I seek the silences how did
All this happen where did this
Come from this wild strange city
This long night of strange people
Strangers strangers strangers
Jungle creatures talking
Jungle talk jungle insects
Jungle beasts wild eyes there is
No escape only this secret scurrying
I understand henceforth every
Cockroach approach the
Scuttling disappearing I am
Familiar with the world of spray
With swatters what escape in this
Buzzing of flies in these
Patterns the air creates for them
Buzz buzz buzz buzz there is
Dance of web spider flea there is
This hole in which I crouch
Conspicuous in my craving for
A cloak of invisibility, imprisoned by
The eyes, the stars, within and without,
The constellations I reached and denied
With the denial by which I am denied

I am cut off I have
Trampled a universe I have
Transgressed the law of holiness
I have eaten the blood
It is *my* blood
Is it not my blood?
Those watery red tissues in glass bottle
Bits of debris, flotsam, fish skin
Is this my child drowning in a
Fiery sea this sudden tidal wave
This rush of mud over Pompeii
Can you hear the rushing child, this world
Is not for you, nor you not yet, for it
Nor I, we are dust, lint, speck, food for
Vacuum cleaners, we are blood together
In a maelstrom of Leviticus we are
Flushed out of caves in Moreau's island

Baby baby it is finished now
But stay with me stay in this
Perfect world let me keep you
Alive let me hold your warm
Body let me baby keep you
From the arguments this time, the schools, the
Newspapers it's a friendly woods we
Walk in on grass as soft as quilts
We are together in this deep soft trap
This well, this long falling I
Tripped the latch with my own hand
I have not stumbled I have rushed
Headlong towards the breakers
Carrying you tossing you from cliffs
I have burnt you on many altars
Offered you to the village elders
For their evening meals, my ram-child,
My Isaac without a saving God—

It is my faith that died
Long before you were conceived
And my ice covered legs move more
Slowly now it is the love law
We must yet obey and how have I loved you?

Euclid was it child of your spirit
Hovering round my moon hollowed night
Is it your ears I have deafened
And your dead universe now
In which I pray. Euclid the books tell us
The place of your birth is uncertain.
I confess I could not have stood
Your craving for perfection
Where did you go so quickly were you so
Uninsistent on life you died so easily
Could you not have fought a little at the oven door
Performed a mere Daniel in a den
Could you not convince me or this
Italian doctor, my accomplice, your father,
My accomplice, could you not through
The long wrestling night of excuses and lies
Shout down the executioner with his
'Life must die that life might live'
Was it you, Euclid, arguing with the moon?
Do you weight me now?

The tides do not return the beaches
Fill with harpooned whales
Cupid as harpoon king grows weary
And sleeps amid poisoned spears
Jonah lies rotting in the store-room
Nineveh is lost. You were
A small fish struggling for three minutes
On the prongs of a well aimed hook
Are you somewhere now Euclid?
Was your angel not yet assigned?
Did we throw you back?

We swam upstream and discovered
The river was an eddy in a larger stream
The choices were ripples in a waterfall
The ripples fell like Niagara
How many stars drowned today
How many possibilities have been denied

My dream daemon leaves my night watching
But the waiting will return to the silences
The rainbow was a promise of fire
But new signs follow the holocaust
There are patterns more hidden than our patterning
Deaths more lasting than our murdering
There are celebrations still in the surety of death
And more resurrections than I have known

Friday. July 71. Ottawa.
"Dear Euclid," the dead moon has announced
"I am indestructible.
 I am star."